PLAYING WITH PARALLEL PORT.

(MAKE YOUR OWN GUI WITH TURBO C TO CONTROL YOUR ROBOT).

"Learn and Make Edition" - G.S.Lab.

By

Ujash.G.Patel

PLAYING WITH PARALLEL PORT.

(MAKE YOUR OWN GUI WITH TURBO C TO CONTROL YOUR ROBOT)

For more detail contact Author - P.ujash@yahoo.com.

Publisher - G.S.Lab.

Series Title - "Learn and Make "

Cover Design - Ms Palak Patel.

Technical Reviewer - Steve Johnson.

Content Writer - Ms Dhara Raval.

ISBN-13: 978-1532834820

ISBN-10: 1532834829

About Author

 Ujash Patel is a Mechatronics engineer, and blogger. He has a bachelor degree in Mechatronics engineering, and a diploma in Mechatronics engineering. He has more than 2 year of Researching and Industrial experience in domain of Mechatronics engineering. After finishing his graduation he served as Tool Room engineer for almost 1 year. He has curiosity in field of Robotics and Mechatronics since childhood. He pursues his interest as individual Researching on Robotics and Mechatronics system.

"**PLAYING WITH PARALLEL PORT**" is second book of Ujash Patel. It is series title of "Learn and Make ".His area of interest includes Mechatronics system, Robotics system, 3d printed Humanoid Robot, Hydraulic and Pneumatic automation.

ACKNOWLEGEMENT

I couldn't have written a book like this without help of lots of People. I would like to thanks **MS Dhara Raval** For working on Introduction Chapters of this book. Many thanks to **MS Palak Patel** for Design My book Cover Page. Finally I would like to thank my Family & Friends for supporting me.

WHOM IS THIS BOOK FOR?

I wrote about the parallel port and its interface. Parallel port is not a common interface port. That is almost replaced by USB or serial port. Still parallel port is easy to interface and program with c language. This book is ideal for beginner in Robotics and Pc Based controlling system. The book Have everything to play with parallel port with personal computer. This is a first book of my Series title **"Learn and Make "**. What is the best title to start my learn and make series other than Playing with parallel port? I start with c language and GUI interface. This is ideal for Beginner to put feet on Robotics. The book is design to fulfilled Requirement of Real practical book.

Preface

Turn your computer in to super controlling device to control Dc, Stepper motor with your own GUI (Graphics User Interface) in turbo c. This book deals with a c language and parallel port communication. The book is design to Learn Development of GUI (Graphics User Interface) with c language. Book contents 6 chapters with step by step guide to learn basic program with turbo c. the book does not contain any of theory explanation on c language and its programming. It's give you practical understanding about GUI Development , Making of Motor Driven Circuit , controlling Dc , Stepper Motor in Real Time Application With your Own Made Operation Window in C .

The book is for

Students, non it engineers, Robotic researcher

What you will learn

1. Development of GUI for controlling 7 led in different sequence.

2. Development of GUI for Controlling Dc motor.

3. Development of GUI for Controlling Stepper motor.

4. Making of Motor driven circuit.

5. Making of Prototype with parallel port and turbo c.

Contents

Chapter 1. Introduction to C language

When I was kid computer is not a common device in 90's. I have always curiosity to find computer behaviour. How its work? What is fundamental formula for that? In Today's world computer is common for everyone. I am surprised to see some of children program their first computer with Raspberry pie. This is all about flow of technology. As per my opinion "**computer is a device which is program to make human life more efficient**". So we have a first question on board what is program. Or what is programming language?

1.1. What is Computer Language?

A computer language is a set of Rules, conventions, Logic, Algorithms used to convey the information to a computer. There are three type of computer language.

1. Machine level Language.

2. Low Level Language.

3. High Level Language.

Machine Level Language - It contains binary string. Which have 0's and 1's that specifies an operation and identifies memory location involved in operation.

Low Level Language - in Low Level Language Software first translate the specified operation symbol to machine language which is understand by computer.

Example- Assembly language.

High Level Language - instruction are given to a computer by using a convenient letter, symbol rather than 0's and 1's.

Example - Pascal.

Where the C Language Stands?

C language was developed in 1970's by Dennis Ritchie at bell laboratories, c language in between the Low Level Language and High Level Language. It's called a middle level language. Which fulfilled the both the criteria of high and low level language.

Over the year c language become flexible in different area of application. In today's modern control system c language is source language to program micro controller or microprocessor in different application.

1.2. General overview of C language and Development system.

1. C is most popular computer programming language.

2. C is unique in programming language in that its provides the conveniences of High and Low level languages.

3. C compile can generate fast code compare to other languages.

4. Its well structured and modular language then other programming language.

5. C language IDE is most users Friendly then most other languages.

Turbo C Development System Contains -

1. IDE (integrated Development Environment).
2. Command Line Development.

1. IDE (integrated Development Environment) it is a screen display with windows and pulls down menus the Program, listing its output error and messages and other information are displayed in separate windows.

Command line development - in command line development editing , compiling ,debugging , linking & program execution are invoked from dos line prompt .

File used in C Program Development

1. Executable file

2. Library & Runtime file.

3. Header File.

4. Programmable.

1. Executable file – This files stores in sub directory BIN. The Most important executable file for turbo c is TC.EXE.

The bin directory also contains

TCC	Command line compiler.
T LINK	Command line liker.
TC INST	Customize Turbo IDE.
CPP	Pre-processor Utility.
T LIB	Library File Manager.
MAKE	File management Program .

2. Runtime Files - various Files are combined with your programs. They are stored in LIB sub Directory. Those are Runtimes Files.

Library Files - Library files are group of precompiled routines for performing specific task. Example -print f().

3. Header files - The sub directory called include contain Header Files. Each Header File Has an ".h" extension.

#include<stdio.h>

#include<iostream.h>

#include<math.h>

#include<dos.h>

#include<graphics.h>

1.3. The Basic Structure of C .

1. Function definition.

2. Delimited.

3. Statement terminator.

4. The Print f () Function.

1. Function Definition - main () is always First function to be executed and is the one which passed when program is executed.

2. Delimited - It following the function definition are the braces which indicate the beginning and ending body of function.

Opening -"{"

Closing - "}"

3. Statement terminator - a statement in c language is terminated with a semicolon ";".

Sample Program

```
#include<stdio.h>

#include<conio.h>

Void main ()

{

printf(" My First Program..!?");

getch();  }
```

Chapter2. Implementation of Different Logic Loop Function with c.

In this chapter we are going to learn about different Logic loop function implementation with C.

LOOP:

Loop Statement used to write Repeat group of statement until a certain condition is reached.

2.1. FOR LOOP
Description:

For loop is Predefined loop structure in which number of iteration is identified. For Loop executes a sequence of statements multiple times. For loop manage their loop variable.

Syntax:

For (Initialization; condition; increment / decrement)
{
Body Of For Loop
}

Initialization: initialization is assignment statement which is use to assign loop variable.

Condition: condition is expression which determines when the loop exists.

Increment / Decrement: When loop is repeated then this will change (add or minus) loop variable.

Flow chart:

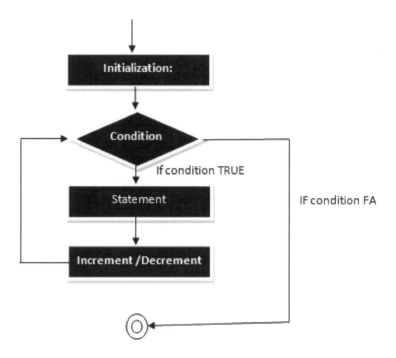

Firstly we will initialize the Loop variable value. Each time condition is check if the condition is true then it will enter in to iteration otherwise it will exit loop. After each iteration, the increment decrement made changes on loop variable.

Example:

```
1) for( ; ; )
    {
     printf(" loop will run forever");
    }
```

In above example, loop will go on infinity looping.

```
2) for ( int m= 0 ; m < 5 ; m++)
    {
     printf( " value of m : %d " , m++);
    }
```

In above example , we have initialize loop variable m to 0 and each time it check condition if m value is less than 5 or not, if the this condition is true then it will print value of m and increment the m value and this process continuation repeat until the m value is not less than 5.

```
3) for (int m=0; m<=10; m++)
   {
       for (int n=0; n<=10; n++)
       {
           printf("%d, %d",m ,n);
       }
   }
```

In the above example is for nested loop this is called nesting of loops. This type of nesting is frequently used for handling multidimensional arrays or printing triangle structure.

4) for (m=1,n=1;m<5 && n<5; m++, n++)

In above example we have initialized two variables. Both variable is separated by commas (,) more than one condition are separated by AND (&&), OR (||) logical operator, increment and decrement is also separated by commas (,).

2.2. While Loop.

While loop is entry control loop. In Single Line loop statement --_Opening and Closing bracket are not needed .In while loop conditional check first, if the condition is true then it will enter into loop otherwise the loop is existed. Initialization, Increment / Decrement and Condition steps are written on different lines

Syntax:

Initialization of variable
 While (Condition)
{
Body of While Loop
Increment / decrement
}

Initialization: initialization is assignment statement which is use to assign loop variable.

Condition: condition is expression which determines when the loop exists.

Increment / Decrement: When loop is repeated then this will change (add or minus) loop variable.

Flow chart:

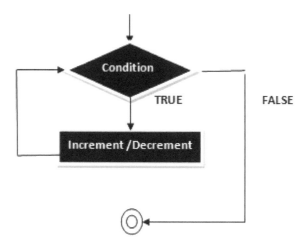

In while Loop, Firstly check Condition, if the condition is true then it will enter into loop otherwise it will exist the loop.

Example:

```
1) while(1)
   {
   printf("loop will run forever ");
   }
```

This will go on infinite loop because every time condition will be true.

```
2) int m=10;
   while(m>5);  //Note it Carefully
   printf("Hiii");
```

It won't print anything .As above loop has sem icolon immediate after the condition statement which shows that loops doesn't have body so no statement will executed.

3) Int m=1;
   while(m < 5)
      {
      printf("value of a: %d", m);
      m++;
      }

In above example , we have initialize loop variable m to 1 and each time it check condition if m value is less than 5 or not, if the this condition is true then it will print value of m and increment the m value and this process continuation repeat until the m value is not less than 5.

4) while(m !=10 ||n >= m)
More than one condition are separated by AND (&&), OR (||) logical operator

2.3. Do While Loop.

Do While loop is exit control loop .In Single Line loop statement --_Opening and Closing bracket are not needed .In do while loop conditional check at last, body of loop is tested at least once, after executing body of loop , it will check if the condition is true then it will enter into loop otherwise the loop is existed. Initialization, Increment / Decrement and Condition steps are written on different lines

Syntax:

Initialization of variable
 Do
{
Body of do While Loop
Increment / decrement
} While (Condition);

Initialization: initialization is assignment statement which is use to assign loop variable.

Condition: condition is expression which determines when the loop exists.

Increment / Decrement: When loop is repeated then this will change (add or minus) loop variable.

Do...while is must terminate with semi colon (;) while other loop doesn't terminated with semicolon

Flow chart:

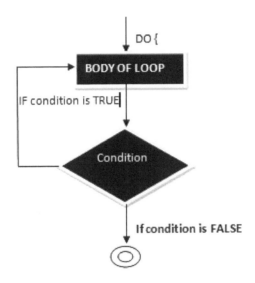

Example:

1) do
   {
   printf("loop will run forever ");
   } while(1);

This will goes on infinite loop because every time condition will be true.

```
2) int m=10;
   do {
     printf ("Hiii \n");
            }while ( m>5);
```

It will print Hi until the condition in while state ment becomes false.

```
3) Int m=1;
   do
       {
     printf("value of m: %d", m);
      m++;
     } while ( m < 5 );
```

In above example, we have initialize loop variable m to 1, first time it all the statement under do loop will execute and then each time it check condition if m value is less than 5 or not, if the this condition is true then it will print value of m and increment the m value and this process continuation repeat until the m value is not less than 5.

Do

{

Printf("value of m: %d , n:%d",m,n);

 }while(m !=10 ||n >= m)

More than one condition are separated by AND (&&), OR (||) logical operator

2.4. IF Else Condition.

The if, if...else statement are used to make decisions in C Programming, that is, to execute some code and ignore some code depending on condition.

IF statement:

If statement check whether the condition is true or not, if condition is true then it will enter into if statement body otherwise if statement body will ignored.

Syntax :

If (condition)

{

// Body of if statement

}

Flowchart:

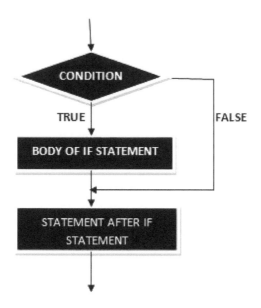

Example:

1) int n = 10 ;
   If(n >= 10)
   {
      Printf (" n is = %d ",n);
   }

In above statement, if statement check whether condition is true or not. If true then it will execute if statement body otherwise statement inside if will ignored.

IF ... else statement:

If...Else statement is executed in situation in which we want to execute some statement when condition is true and execute other statement if condition will false.

Syntax :

If (condition)

{

// Body of if statement

}

Else

{

//body of else

}

Flowchart:

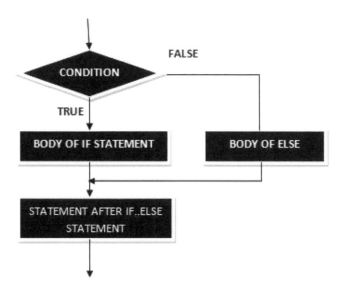

Example:

1) int n = 10 ;
```
   If( n >= 10 )
   {
     Printf ( " n is = %d ",n);
   }
   Else
   {
     Printf( " n value is less than 10 ");
   }
```

In above statement, if statement check whether condition is true or not. If true then it will execute if statement body otherwise it will execute else body.

Switch Case:
Switch case is similar as if statement, in switch case can have multiple conditions. Switch case is mostly used when we have more than one choice and we need different statement execute on each choice.

Syntax:

switch(choice)

{

case choice1 :

body of case 1 ;

break;

case choice2:

body of case 2;

break;

case choicen:

body of case n;

```
break;

default :

body of default case;

}
```

Flowchart:

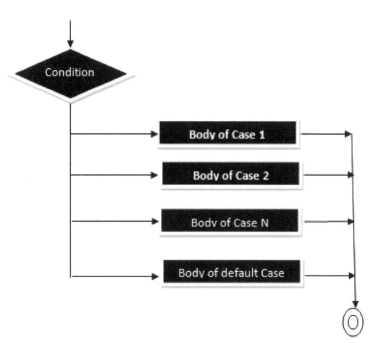

Example :

```
Int day = 3 ;
Switch(day)
{
Case 1 :
Printf (" Sunday ");
Break;
Case 2 :
Printf (" Monday ");
Break;
Case 3:
Printf (" Tuesday ");
Break;
Case 4 :
Printf (" Wednesday ");
Break;
Case 5 :
Printf (" Thursday");
Break;
Case 6 :
Printf (" Friday ");
Break;
Case 7 :
Printf (" Saturday ");
Break;
Default :
Printf("invalid choice ")
}
```

In above example, we have set day value is 3, and pass this value on switch case condition, switch case match their corresponding case and execute that block. In our example day int is 3 so it will execute case 3 and print Tuesday as output. Break statement after each case is used to terminate case and go out of switch case. If no case is match on choice then default case will execute.

Chapter 3. Implementation of basic Graphics with C.

In this chapter we are going to learn graphics development with c. so let's see some of the example of generating line, circle, shapes, and rectangle with c program.

3.1 sample program to draw straight line.

Before start programming we have to do some basic calculation about straight line. Let's consider one straight line which has a coordinates A and B. So we have to define its starting and ending position on screen. So sub coordinate must be described as X1, X2, Y1, Y2.

Understand Coordinate system

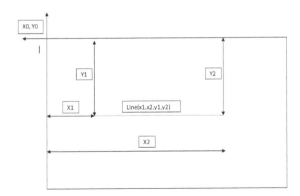

Program to draw Straight Line

```c
#include<stdio.h>
#include<graphics.h>
#include<conio.h>
main()
{
int gd=DETECT,gm,x1,x2,y1,y2;
initgraph(&gd,&gm,"c:\\tc\\bgi ");
setbkcolor(3);      //For background color
setcolor(8);        //For output grafics color
printf("Enter the starting point of line :");
scanf("%d%d",&x1,&y1);
printf("Enter the end point of line :");
scanf("%d%d",&x2,&y2);
line(x1,y1,x2,y2);
closegraph();
getch();
return 0; }
```

Program to Draw Rectangle using line

```c
#include<stdio.h>
#include<graphics.h>
#include<conio.h>
main()
{
int gd=DETECT,gm,x1,x2,x3,x4,y1,y2,y3,y4;
clrscr();                          //Clear   screen
initgraph(&gd,&gm,"c:\\tc\\bgi ");
setbkcolor(4);      //For background color
setcolor(1);       //For output grafics color
printf("Enter top left point of rectangle :");
scanf("%d%d",&x1,&y1);
printf("Enter bottom right point of rectangle :");
scanf("%d%d",&x3,&y3);     x2=x3;     y2=y1;
x4=x1; y4=y3;
line(x1,y1,x2,y2);
line(x2,y2,x3,y3);
```

```
line(x3,y3,x4,y4);

line(x4,y4,x1,y1);

getch();

closegraph();

getch();

return 0;

}
```

3.2 sample program to draw circle.

```
#include<stdio.h>

#include<conio.h>

#include<graphics.h>

main()

{

int gd=DETECT,gm,h,k,r;

clrscr();

initgraph(&gd,&gm,"c:\\tc\\bgi ");

setbkcolor(2);

setcolor(6);
```

```c
printf("Enter the  center of circle :");

scanf("%d%d",&h,&k);

printf("Enter the radious of circle :");

scanf("%d",&r);

circle(h,k,r);

getch();

closegraph();

getch();

return 0;

}
```

Program for circle animation

```c
#include<stdio.h>

#include<graphics.h>

#include<math.h>

#include<dos.h>

#include<conio.h>

main()

{
```

```c
float h,k,r,i;

int gd=DETECT,gm;

initgraph(&gd,&gm," c:\\tc\\bgi");

setbkcolor(8);

setcolor(5);

for(i=1;i<=300;i++)

{

circle(250,250,i); delay(10);

}

getch();

closegraph();

getch();

return 0;

}
```

Program for multiple circles

```c
#include<stdio.h>

#include<conio.h>

#include<dos.h>
```

```c
#include<math.h>

#include<graphics.h>

main()

{

int gd=DETECT,gm,x,y,i,j,m,n;

clrscr();

initgraph(&gd,&gm,"c:\\tc\\bgi ");

printf("Enter number of raw & colom :");

scanf("%d%d",&n,&m);

k=20;

l=20;

 for(i=0;i<=n;i++)

{

for(j=0;j<=m;j++)

 {

circle(x,y,10);

 x=x+20;

 }
```

```c
 y=y+20;

 x=20;

 }
closegraph();

getch();

return 0;

}
```

Animation of line in circle

```c
#include<stdio.h>

#include<math.h>

#include<graphics.h>

#include<dos.h>

#include<conio.h>

main()

{

int gd=DETECT,gm,j;

float h,k,r,i,m,n;

initgraph(&gd,&gm,"c:\\tc\\bgi ");
```

```c
printf("Enter the center :");

scanf("%f%f",&h,&k);

printf("Enter the radius :");

scanf("%f",&r);

circle(h,k,r);

line(h,k,h+r,k);

j=6; for(i=1;i<=200;i++) { m=r*cos(j); n=r*sin(j);

line(h,k,h+m,k-n);

j=j+6;

delay(100);

}

closegraph();

getch();

return 0;

}
```

3.3.Program for small cad software in c.

```c
#include<stdio.h>

#include<graphics.h>

#include<conio.h>

#include<dos.h>

#include<math.h>

main()

{

int gd=DETECT,gm,j,i;

float x1,x2,x3,x4,y1,y2,y3,y4,h,k,r;

char w; initgraph(&gd,&gm,"c:\\tc\\bgi ");

setbkcolor(3);

setcolor(11);

start: printf("Enter the chooise");

rintf("\nEnter 1 for line");

printf("\nEnter 2 for rectangle");

printf("\nEnter 3 for circle   ");
```

42

```c
printf("\nEnter 4 for retangle animation");
printf("\nEnter 5 for circle animation  :");
scanf("%d",&j);
switch(j)
{
case 1:
printf("Enter the first point :");
scanf("%f%f",&x1,&y1);
printf("Enter the end point :");
scanf("%f%f",&x2,&y2);
 line(x1,y1,x2,y2);
break;
case 2:
printf("Enter the top left corner :");
scanf("%f%f",&x1,&y1);
printf("Enter the bottom right corner :");
scanf("%f%f",&x3,&y3);
rectangle(x1,y1,x3,y3);
```

```c
break;
case 3:
printf("Enter the center :");
scanf("%f%f",&h,&k);
printf("Enter radius :");
scanf("%f",&r);
circle(h,k,r);
break;
case 4:
printf("Enter the top left corner :");
scanf("%f%f",&x1,&y1);
printf("Enter the bottom right corner :");
scanf("%f%f",&x3,&y3);
rectangle(x1,y1,x3,y3);
for(i=1;i<=100;i++)
{
rectangle(x1-i,y1-i,x3+i,y3+i);
delay(100);
```

```c
}
break;
case 5:
printf("Enter the center :");
scanf("%f%f",&h,&k);
printf("Enter radius :");
scanf("%f",&r);
for(i=1;i<=100;i++)
{
circle(h,k,r+i);
delay(100);
}
break;
}
printf("Do you want to continue?(y/n)");
scanf("%s",&w);
if(w=='y'
)
```

```c
{
goto start;
}
if(w=='n')
{
goto end;
 }
end:
closegraph();
getch();
return 0;
}
```

3.5. Program for mouse interface in c.

```c
#include<stdio.h>

#include<math.h>

#include<graphics.h>

#include<dos.h>

#include<conio.h>
```

```
union REGS i,o;

main()

{

intgd=DETECT,gm;
initgraph(&gd,&gm,"c:\\tc\\bgi ");

i.x.ax=1;

int86(0x33,&i,&o);

closegraph();

getch();

return 0;

}
```

Program to limit curser to mouse

```
#include<stdio.h>

#include<math.h>

#include<graphics.h>

#include<dos.h>

#include<conio.h>

union REGS i,o;
```

```
main()

{

intgd=DETECT,gm;
initgraph(&gd,&gm,"c:\\tc\\bgi ");

rectangle(100,100,400,400);

i.x.ax=1;

int86(0x33,&i,&o);

i.x.ax=7;

int86(0x33,&i,&o);

i.x.cx=100; i.x.dx=400;

int86(0x33,&i,&o);

i.x.ax=8;

int86(0x33,&i,&o);

i.x.cx=100;

i.x.dx=400;

int86(0x33,&i,&o);

closegraph();

getch();
```

```
return 0;

}
```

3.6. Program for Free Hand Sketch.

```
#include <graphics.h>

#include <dos.h>

union REGS i,o;

main()

{

int gd=DETECT,gm,button,x1,y1,x2,y2;

initgraph(&gd,&gm,"c:\\tc\\bgi");

i.x.ax=0; int86(0x33,&i,&o);

if(o.x.ax==0)

{

printf("No Mouse is available..");

exit();

restorecrtmode();

}
```

```c
outtextxy(230,400,"Press any key to exit....");

while(!kbhit())

{

show_mouse();

get_mouse_pos(&x1,&y1,&button);

x2=x1; y2=y1;

while(button==1)

 {

 hide_mouse();

line(x1,y1,x2,y2);

x1=x2; y1=y2;

get_mouse_pos(&x2,&y2,&button);

}

 }

restorecrtmode();

 }

show_mouse()

{
```

```
i.x.ax=1; int86(0x33,&i,&o);

}

 hide_mouse()

{

i.x.ax=2; int86(0x33,&i,&o);

 }

get_mouse_pos(int *x,int *y,int *button)

{

i.x.ax=3; int86(0x33,&i,&o);

*x=o.x.cx;

*y=o.x.dx;

*button=o.x.bx&1;

}
```

3.7. Small cad software using mouse.

```
#include<stdio.h>

#include<graphics.h>

#include<dos.h>

#include<conio.h>
```

```c
union REGS i,o;

main()

{

int
gd=DETECT,gm,x,y,cl,x1,x2,x3,x4,y1,y2,y3,y4,h,k,r;

initgraph(&gd,&gm,"c:\\tc\\bgi ");

rectangle(10,20,100,60);

gotoxy(3,3);

printf("LINE");

rectangle(110,20,200,60);

gotoxy(16,3);

printf("RECTANGLE");

rectangle(210,20,300,60);

gotoxy(28,3);

printf("CIRCLE");

i.x.ax=1;

int86(0x33,&i,&o);
```

```
do

{

i.x.ax=3;

int86(0x33,&i,&o);

x=o.x.cx;

y=o.x.dx; cl=o.x.bx;

if(10<x&&x<100&&20<y&&y<60&&cl==1)

{

printf("\nEter start point:");

scanf("%d%d",&x1,&y1);

printf("Eter end point:");

scanf("%d%d",&x2,&y2);

line(x1,y1,x2,y2); }

if(100<x&&x<200&&20<y&&y<60&&cl==1)

{

printf("\nEter top left corner:");

scanf("%d%d",&x3,&y3);

printf("Eter bottom right corner:");
```

```c
scanf("%d%d",&x4,&y4);

rectangle(x3,y3,x4,y4);

}

if(210<x&&x<300&&20<y&&y<60&&cl==1)

{

printf("\nEter the center:");

scanf("%d%d",&h,&k);

printf("Eter radius:");

 scanf("%d",&r);

circle(h,k,r);

}}

while(!kbhit());

closegraph();

getch();

return 0;

}
```

Chapter 4. Introduction to Embedded C and Parallel Port Programming.

First three chapter of this book is all about introduction of c language programming. Let's try to understand embedded system.

4.1. What is embedded system?

Embedded system is an electro mechanic system. This is design to perform more than one task at a time. The embedded system is a unique word. It can be in any form of device. It can be Micro processing unit, it can be microcontroller system, or it can be your computing system.

Computer itself an embedded unit. Which have power to control external devices, Interface input device. So next 3 chapters we will going to learn how to use your computer as an embedded system which control your motor (final device) in real time application.

What is embedded c?

As we discuss in earlier chapter turbo c is integrated development environment. This gives flexibility to programmer for interfacing outer device, controlling outer device with turbo c. This unique feature of turbo c gives power to convert computer to embedded computing system which is capable to control external hardware.

4.2. Introduction to Parallel Port.

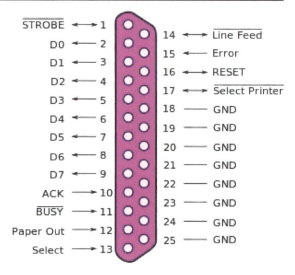

A parallel port is 25 pin connector which is used to send and receive several bit at a time with more than one wire. Parallel port is known as a DB 25.

How to identify parallel Port?

Just look backside of your pc you will find a 25 pins female connector which is generally used for printer interface.

Mode of parallel port

The computer is capable to run parallel port on different mode depending on application and available resourcing. This can be classifying under 6 different categories.

1. Centroid

It is also defended as IEEE 1284 and is backward compatible with unidirectional mode. This mode is capable of transmitting 150 kbps.

2. Nibble mode

Introduced by Hewlett Packard. Nibble mode is allowing device to use four lines of compatibility mode while transmitting data 4 bit at time.

This mode is generally used with centroid mode which used for enhanced printer status.

3. Uni-Direction mode

Use to transmit and receive data at a time. it can be used for only one direction purpose . This port was found before 1995, capable of transmitting four bit at a time.

4. Bi Directional

Capable to communicate data both direction this mode was first introduced by ibm in 1987 .bidirectional port is an 8 bit port capable of transmitting 75 to 300kbps.

5. EPP

Enhance parallel port that works almost twice as fast as earlier mode. It can be transfer data between a peripheral devices and computer at same time. This port was first developed in 1991.

6. ECP

Enhanced capabilities port. Developed by Microsoft and Hewlett Packard and announced in 1992. It is capable of transmitting of up to 2 mbps & it had a FIFO buffer up to 16 byte.

4.3. Addition information And Pin Description.

SIGNAL	BIT	PIN	DIRECTION	VALUE
-Strobe	¬C0	1	Output	-
+Data Bit 0	D0	2	Output	1
+Data Bit 1	D1	3	Output	2
+Data Bit 2	D2	4	Output	4
+Data Bit 3	D3	5	Output	8
+Data Bit 4	D4	6	Output	16
+Data Bit 5	D5	7	Output	32
+Data Bit 6	D6	8	Output	64
+Data Bit 7	D7	9	Output	128
-Acknowledge	S6	10	Input	-
+Busy	¬S7	11	Input	-
+Paper End	S5	12	Input	-
+Select In	S4	13	Input	-
-Auto Feed	¬C1	14	Output	-
-Error	S3	15	Input	-
-Initialize	C2	16	Output	-

Pin 1 – Data Acknowledgement pin.

Pin 2 -9 – Data transfer pin.

Pin 10 – acknowledge that the data has finished processing and when the signal is high.

Pin 11 – when the signal goes high indicate that printer accept data. Once this signal; goes low pin 10 goes high.

Pin 12 – printer paper jam when signal high.

Pin 13 – high – indicating ready to print.

Pin 14 – when low signal pc has indicated that printer insert a line after each line.

Pin 15 – error pin.

Pin 16 – internal reset.

Pin 17 – select input.

Pin 18 – Ground.

What is parallel port use for?

In today's world parallel port is almost replaced with usb port. But there is some Rare application found in printer, scanner, Iomega zip drive where parallel port technology still live. Parallel port is most easy port to interface with outer device. Here in this book we will going to learn how to use data transfer pin p2-p9 for controlling outer device with some motor driven circuit.

Output syntax programming for parallel port

outport(0x378,Value);

Pin 2 – outport(0x378,1);

Pin 3 - outport(0x378,2);

Pin 4 - outport(0x378,4);

Pin 5 - outport(0x378,8);

Pin 6 - outport(0x378,16);

Pin 7 - outport(0x378,32);

Pin 8 - outport(0x378,64);

Pin 9 - outport(0x378,128);

Chapter 5. Playing Light Emitting Diode.

5.1. What is Light emitting Diode?

A Light Emitting diode is semiconductor device that emits light when current passes thought it. A led consists of two element P type and N Type semiconductor. These two element forming region called P-N Junction.

How Led Works?

When a diode is forward biased so that electrode & holes are forth across the junction. They are constant combining with each other after electrode moves from the N type to P type silicon. It will combine with a hole and disappear. That makes atom complete and gives off burst of energy in form of light.

1. N type silicon has extra electrons.

2. P type silicon has extra Holes.

3. When Battery is connected across the P-N Junction.

4. Electrode& holes cross the junction and combine.

5. Particle of light given off as hole and electrode recombine.

How to Identify LED Terminal?

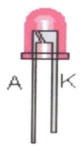

We can identify the LED terminal With Visual observation. Long leg of LED known ad Anode While Short Leg of LED Known as Cathode.

Electrical Symbol

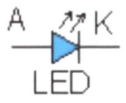

LED used in Several Electronics application. Most effective use of Led as a program checking circuit. We can use Led circuit to check program sequence (output checker). And it's a basic interface to know about output interface with any microcontroller so let's start with led here.

5.2. Control Multiple Led With Turbo C and Parallel Port.
Part to be Required.

1. Bread board

2. Jumper wires

3. LED (Light Emitting Diode).

Circuit diagram

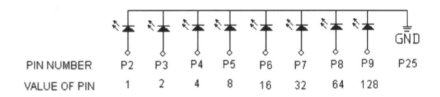

PIN NUMBER	P2	P3	P4	P5	P6	P7	P8	P9	P25
VALUE OF PIN	1	2	4	8	16	32	64	128	

Bread Board circuit

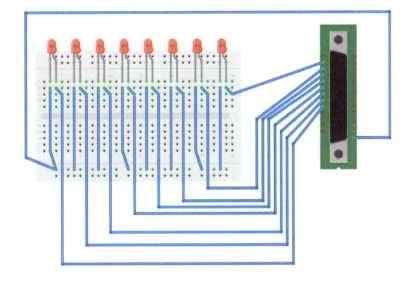

With the help of soldering Iron solder the jumper wire on male connector parallel port as shown in breadboard circuit.

Plug parallel port to pc. Now we have everything is ready to start with first interface with turbo c.

Program to blink individual Led in sequence – forward direction.

```c
#include<stdio.h>

#include<dos.h>

#include<conio.h>

#include<math.h>

void main()

{

int i; for(i=0;i<=7;i++)

{

outport(0x378,pow(2,i));

delay(1000);

outport(0x378,0);

delay(500);

}

getch();

}
```

Program to blink individual led in sequence –Reverse direction

```c
#include<stdio.h>
#include<dos.h>
#include<conio.h>
#include<math.h>
#include<graphics.h>
Void main()
{
int i; for(i=0;i<=8;i++)
{
outport(0x378,pow(2,i));
delay(10);
outport(0x378,0);
delay(10);
}
getch();
}
```

5.3 Making of Visual Interface to control individual LED.

Program

```c
#include<stdio.h>

#include<graphics.h>

#include<dos.h>

#include<conio.h>

union REGS i,o;

main()

{

int gd=DETECT,gm,x,y,cl;

clrscr();

initgraph(&gd,&gm,"c:\\tc\\bgi ");

rectangle(10,60,50,110);

gotoxy(3,6);

printf("LED1");

rectangle(60,60,100,110);

gotoxy(9,6);
```

68

```c
printf("LED2");

rectangle(110,60,150,110);

gotoxy(15,6);

printf("LED3");

rectangle(160,60,200,110);

gotoxy(22,6);

printf("LED4");

rectangle(210,60,250,110);

 gotoxy(28,6);

printf("LED5");

rectangle(260,60,300,110);

gotoxy(34,6);

printf("LED6");

rectangle(310,60,350,110);

 gotoxy(40,6);

printf("LED7");

rectangle(360,60,400,110);

gotoxy(47,6);
```

```
printf("LED8");

i.x.ax=1;

int86(0x33,&i,&o);

do

{

i.x.ax=3; int86(0x33,&i,&o);

x=o.x.cx; y=o.x.dx;

cl=o.x.bx;

if(10<x&&x<50&&60<y&&y<110&&cl==1)

{

outport(0x378,1);

 }

if(60<x&&x<100&&60<y&&y<110&&cl==1)

{

 outport(0x378,2);

}

if(110<x&&x<150&&60<y&&y<110&&cl==1)

 {
```

```
outport(0x378,4);

}

if(160<x&&x<200&&60<y&&y<110&&cl==1)

{

outport(0x378,8);

}

if(210<x&&x<250&&60<y&&y<110&&cl==1)

{

outport(0x378,16);

}

if(260<x&&x<300&&60<y&&y<110&&cl==1)

{

outport(0x378,32);

}

if(310<x&&x<350&&60<y&&y<110&&cl==1)

{

outport(0x378,64);

}
```

```
if(360<x&&x<400&&60<y&&y<110&&cl==1)

{

outport(0x378,128);

}}

while(!kbhit());

closegraph();

getch();

return 0;

}
```

Chapter 6. Playing with Dc Motor.

6.1. Introduction to Dc Motor.

DC motor is a direct current motor. An electrical machine which converts dc power to mechanical power it's called dc motor.

Construction

The construction of dc motor contains a current carrying armature which placed in permanent or an electromagnet as shown in diagram.

Working principle

Working of dc motor is depended on the Fleming left hand Rule. Fleming left hand rule says that if we extend the index finger middle finger and thumb of our left hand in such a way that the current caring conductor is placed in magnetic field is perpendicular to the direction of current then the conductor experience a force in the direction mutually perpendicular to both the direction of field and the current in conductor.

$$F = BIL$$

F = force

B = magnetic field Weber /m2.

I= current in ampere

L = coil Length in meter.

There are lots of things that can be considered while selection of dc motor. But there are also lots of Resources on internet to understand that all so let me directly jump to Dc motor controlling.

Control on and off action of dc motor

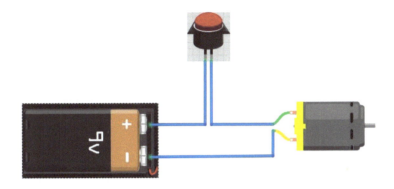

Control direction with 4 switching action

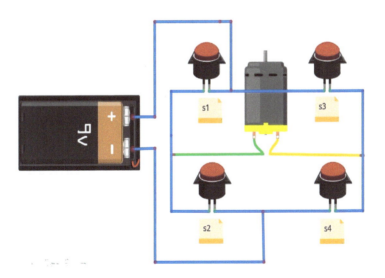

We can control direction of dc motor with switching current position. In above picture there are 4 switches used to control direction of dc motor let's summarized working description with help of simple truth table.

S1	S2	S3	S4	output
1	0	0	1	Clockwise direction
0	1	1	0	Anti clockwise
0	0	0	0	Stop
1	1	1	1	Break (stop)

Just replace all switches with NPN transistor and you will have an H-bridge circuit.

6.3. Control Dc motor With H- Bridge circuit.

H Bridge is transistor base motor driven circuit use to drive dc motor in both the direction. H Bridge is basically switching circuit which provides switching function to control direction of dc motor.

Part to be required

1. NPN transistor

2. Resistor

3. Breadboard circuit4

4. Jumper wires

Breadboard circuit

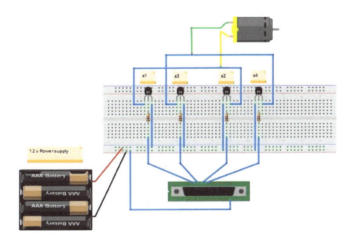

Program

```
#include<stdio.h>

#include<conio.h>

Void main()

{

char j;

clrscr();

printOf("Enter 1 for forward the motor :");

printf("\nEnter 2 for reverse the motor :");

printf("\nEnter 0 for stop the motor :");

do

 {

 j=getche();

 if(k=='1')

 {

 outport(0x378,6);

 }

 if(j=='2')
```

```
{
outport(0x378,9);
 }
 }
while(j!='0');
Outport(0x378,0);
getch();
 }
```

Output of program

1 – Motor will rotate clockwise direction.

2- Motor will rotate anti-clockwise direction.

0 – stop.

6.4. Making of GUI in turbo c to control dc motor with H-Bridge circuit

Program

```c
#include<stdio.h>

#include<conio.h>

#include<graphics.h>

#include<math.h>

#include<dos.h>

union REGS i,o;

main()

{

int gd=DETECT,gm,h,k,r,x,y,cl;

clrscr();

initgraph(&gd,&gm,"c:\\tc\bgi");

setbkcolor(6);

setcolor(2);

rectangle(100,150,200,250);

gotoxy(10,9);
```

```
printf("clockwise");

rectangle(200,150,300,200);

gotoxy(25,9); printf("Anti-clockwise");

rectangle(290,100,390,170);

 gotoxy(41,9);

printf("STOP");

i.x.ax=1; int86(0x33,&i,&o);

 i.x.ax=3;

do { int86(0x33,&i,&o);

 x=o.x.cx;

 y=o.x.dx;

 cl=o.x.bx;

if(50<x&&x<150&&100<y&&y<170&&cl==1)

{

outport(0x378,6);

}

if(170<x&&x<270&&100<y&&y<170&&cl==1)

{
```

```
outport(0x378,9);

}

if(290<x&&x<390&&100<y&&y<170&&cl==1)

{

outport(0x378,0);

}}

while(!kbhit());

getch();

return 0;

}
```

6.5. Control Dc motor with L293d Motor driven and Turbo C.
Introduction to L293d motor driven circuit

L293d is an dual h-bridge motor driven integrated circuit in common mode two dc motor can be driven simultaneously forward and reverse direction.

Note

Enable pin 1 and 9 must be high for motor to start operating in desire direction .

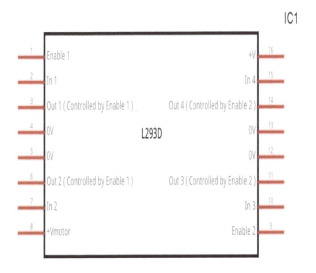

Pin description

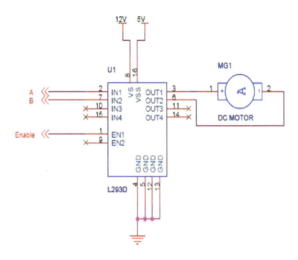

Pin No	Function	Name
1	Enable pin for Motor 1: active high	Enable 1,2
2	Input 1 for Motor 1	Input 1
3	Output 1 for Motor 1	Output 1
4	Ground (0V)	Ground
5	Ground (0V)	Ground
6	Output 2 for Motor 1	Output 2
7	Input 2 for Motor 1	Input 2
8	Supply voltage for Motors: 9-12V (up to 36V)	Vcc_2
9	Enable pin for Motor 2: active high	Enable 3,4
10	Input 1 for Motor 1	Input 3
11	Output 1 for Motor 1	Output 3
12	Ground (0V)	Ground
13	Ground (0V)	Ground
14	Output 2 for Motor 1	Output 4
15	Input2 for Motor 1	Input 4
16	Supply voltage: 5V (up to 36V)	Vcc_1

Program

```
#include<stdio.h>
#include<conio.h>
void main()
{
char j;
clrscr();
printf("Enter 1 for forward the motor :");
printf("\nEnter 2 for reverse the motor :");
printf("\nEnter 3 for stop the motor :");
do
{
j=getche();
if(j=='1')
{
outport(0x378,1);
}
if(j=='2')
```

```
{
outport(0x378,2);
}}
while(j!='0');
Outport(0x378,0);
getch();
}
```

Chapter 7.Playing With Stepper Motor

7.1. What is stepper motor?

Stepper motor is basically a brushless dc motor. It converts full rotation in to number of equal steps. Stepper motor construction has multiple coils that are organized in such a group that called phases. By energize phases in sequence we will get motor rotation. By giving computerized control pulse we can get desire potion and accurate steps which makes stepper motor ideal for Precision Position control system.

Selection of stepper motor

Stepper motor comes in variety of size and specification selection of stepper motor depends on the application Area.

Precision positioning – Stepper motor is Best to move in precision steps, they excellent in application of X, Y Plotter, CNC Machine Drive , some Disc driver , Camera platform .

Speed control – Stepper motor consist of open loop system which moves in desire direction with Given pulse. This specification gives precision speed control benefit to stepper motor.

Low Speed torque – Generally Dc motor have a Low torque at minimum speed. Stepper motor gives high torque at minimum speed .that Makes motor ideal for Low speed High Torque Robotics Application.

Limitation of Stepper motor

Low Efficiency

Limited High Speed Torque

No feedback system

7.2. Basic type of stepper motor

There are two basic type of stepper motor

1.Unipolar Motor

2. Bipolar Motor.

Unipolar stepper motor vs bipolar Motor

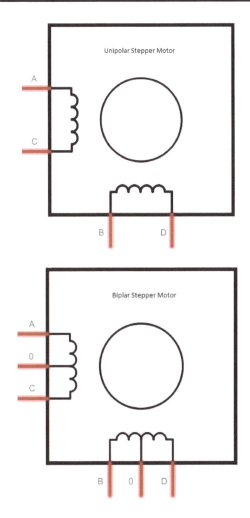

Unipolar Drives always energize the coil in same way. Common Lead will always negative other lead always positive. We can drive unipolar motor with simple transistor logic.

Disadvantage – Less Torque

Bipolar Motor Drives by energizing the phases with alternating the polarity. All the coils can be put to work turning motor.

5 wire Motor

5 wire motor is unipolar type of motor. The entire common coil wires are tied together internally brought out as a 5th wire this can only be driven as unipolar motor.

6 wire Motor

This Motor only joints the common wire of 2 paired Phases. These two wires can be joined to create 5 wires unipolar. We can use it as bipolar motor just ignore common wire.

8 wire motor

It can be driven as a versatile motor.

4 phases unipolar

All the common wires are connected together just like 5 wire motor

2 phases bipolar

If we connect in series like 6 wire motor. Then we can drive it as bipolar motor.

2 phase parallel

Phase connected in parallel. It results half Resistance and inductance.

7.3.Stepper Motor Specification.

Model – 28BYJ-48(unipolar).

Rated voltage – 50vdc.

Phase – 4.

Speed Ratio – 1/64.

Frequency – 100Hz.

Dc Resistance – 500+/- 7%.

Idle in – traction Frequency - >600Hz.

Idle out – traction Frequency - >1000Hz.

Self – Positioning Torque - >34.3mN.m.

Friction Torque – 1200 gf.m(Max)

Insulated Resistance ->10M ohm.

Insulated Resistance -600VAC.

7.4. Pin description ULN 2003.

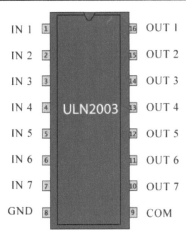

Uln 2003 IC is a high voltage and current Darlington array IC, it have 7 open collector Darlington pairs with common emitter. A pair of Darlington is an arrangement of two bipolar transistors. This IC belongs to the family of ULN 200x Ices.

This ic used as stepper motor driven circuit. The pair of Darlington is esteemed at 500mA and can be withstanding peak current 600mA.the pin i/ps & o/ps are provided reverse to each other. Each driver also has a suppression diode to dissipate voltage while driving inductive load with uln 2003.

Pin No	Function	Name
1	Input for 1st channel	Input 1
2	Input for 2nd channel	Input 2
3	Input for 3rd channel	Input 3
4	Input for 4th channel	Input 4
5	Input for 5th channel	Input 5
6	Input for 6th channel	Input 6
7	Input for 7th channel	Input 7
8	Ground (0V)	Ground
9	Common free wheeling diodes	Common
10	Output for 7th channel	Output 7
11	Output for 6th channel	Output 6
12	Output for 5th channel	Output 5
13	Output for 4th channel	Output 4
14	Output for 3rd channel	Output 3
15	Output for 2nd channel	Output 2
16	Output for 1st channel	Output 1

7.5.Bread board circuit and Wiring Diagram.

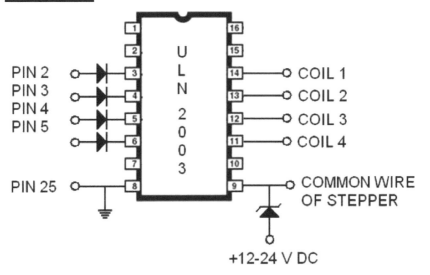

(ULN 2003 Schematic Diagram)

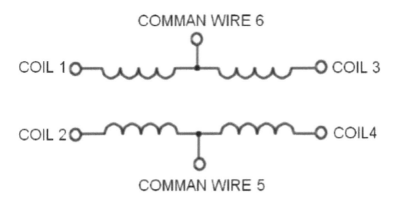

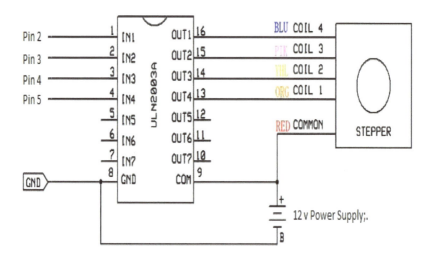

7.6. Program to control stepper motor.

```
#include<stdio.h>

#include<conio.h>

#include<dos.h>

Void main()

{

int i,j,k;

printf("Enter the delay :");

scanf("%d",&i);
```

```c
printf("Enter the number of step :");

scanf("%d",&j);

for(k=1;k<=j;k++)

{

outport(0x378,1);

delay(i);

if(k==j)

{

goto end;

}

k=k+1;

outport(0x378,2);

delay(i);

if(k==j)

{

goto end;

}

k=k+1;
```

```c
outport(0x378,4);

delay(i);

if(k==j)

{

goto end;

} k=k+1;

outport(0x378,8);

delay(i);

if(k==j)

{

goto end;

}}

end:

getch();

}
```

www.ingramcontent.com/pod-product-compliance
Lightning Source LLC
Chambersburg PA
CBHW041152050326
40690CB00001B/445